So merry! So festive! These plastic canvas projects by MizFitz are the jolliest things you can stitch for Christmas. Make a Santa or Reindeer Tissue Box Cover. For the dining table, put Santa's entire sleigh on display. Fashion some very cute ornaments for the tree, or create a panel of Christmas personalities with one of the two character Lineups. What a fun way to add more joy to the season!

About the Designers

John and Rose Fitzgerald of Beloit, Wisconsin are the popular design team known as MizFitz—and as you can see, they love Christmas!

Rose says, "We usually have three Christmas trees, with one of them decorated in our plastic canvas designs. When our kids were young, the whole family was involved in the design business. Our son even made plastic canvas ornaments and sold them."

At Leisure Arts, we're excited about presenting these cheery MizFitz patterns from our library of favorites. Merry Christmas to you and yours, and happy stitching!

Table Of Contents

Santa Tissue Box Cover 2

Reindeer Tissue Box Cover 6

Sleigh Table Decoration 9

Reindeer Ornament 16

Santa Ornament 17

Christmas Lineup 18

Snow Family Lineup 26

General Instructions 34

LEISURE ARTS, INC.
Little Rock, Arkansas

Santa Tissue Box Cover

Size
6³/₄"w x 9¹/₄"h x 5"d
(fits a 4¹/₄"w x 5¹/₄"h x 4¹/₄"d boutique tissue box)

Supplies
Three 10¹/₂" x 13¹/₂" sheets of 7 mesh plastic canvas
Worsted weight yarn
#16 tapestry needle
Two 12mm moving eyes
¹/₂" pink pom-pom
¹/₄" white pom-pom
Clear-drying craft glue

Stitches Used
Alternating Scotch Stitch, French Knot, Gobelin Stitch, Overcast Stitch, and Tent Stitch. Refer to **General Instructions**, pages 35-36, for stitch diagrams.

Instructions
Follow charts to cut and stitch Santa Tissue Box Cover Pieces. Use matching color Overcast Stitches for all joining unless otherwise noted.

Join Sides along long edges. Matching ★'s, join Hat Front to Front and Sides, stitching through three layers of canvas. Use white Overcast Stitches to continue joining Front to Sides.

Matching ✖'s, tack Beard to Front. Tack Mustache and Eyebrows to Front. Glue eyes and pink pom-pom to Front. Join Top to Front and Sides.

Matching ▲'s, join Hat Top to Top. Tack bottom edge (ball area) of Hat Top to Beard.

Join Star pieces along unworked edges. Tack to Hat Top.

For Bird, tack Beak and Wings to Bird pieces; join along unworked edges. Using red Overcast Stitches, join Hat pieces along unworked edges. Place Hat on Bird. Tack Feet to Bird. Tack Feet to Top. Glue white pom-pom to Hat.

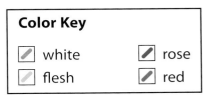

Color Key

▨	white	▨	rose
▨	flesh	▨	red

Front (30 x 38 threads)

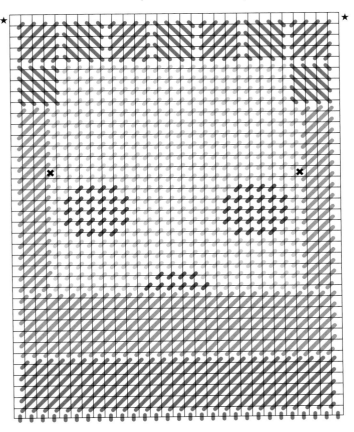

Continued on page 4.

Side (30 x 38 threads) (stitch 3)

Top (30 x 30 threads)

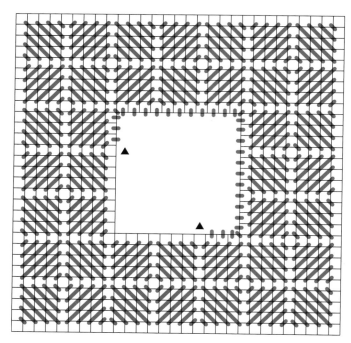

Color Key

⊘	white
⊘	yellow
⊘	red
⊘	dk red
⊘	blue
●	black Fr. Knot

Bird Feet (8 x 8 threads)

Beak (4 x 4 threads)

Bird Front (17 x 17 threads)

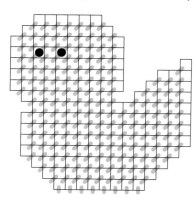

Bird Back (17 x 17 threads)

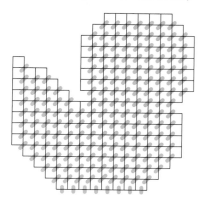

Back Wing (11 x 6 threads)

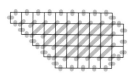

Front Wing (11 x 6 threads)

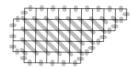

Bird Hat Front (13 x 8 threads)

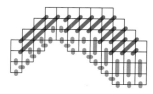

Bird Hat Back (13 x 8 threads)

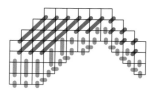

Eyebrows (5 x 4 threads each)

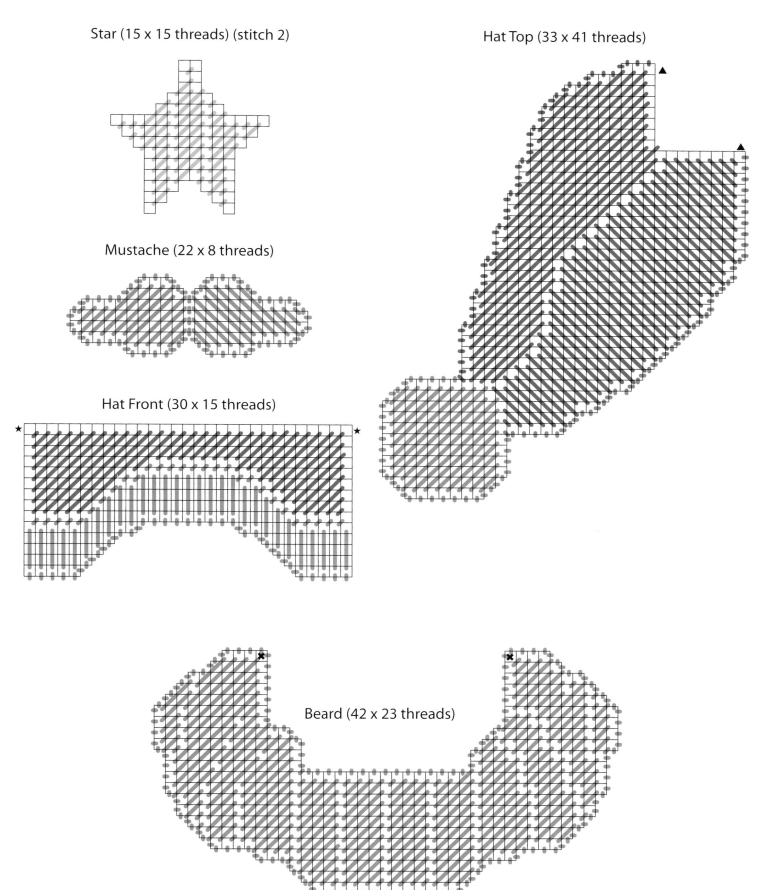

Star (15 x 15 threads) (stitch 2)

Hat Top (33 x 41 threads)

Mustache (22 x 8 threads)

Hat Front (30 x 15 threads)

Beard (42 x 23 threads)

Reindeer Tissue Box Cover

Size
6¹/₄"w x 11¹/₂"h x 4³/₄"d
(fits a 4¹/₄"w x 5¹/₄"h x 4¹/₄"d boutique tissue box)

Supplies
Two 10¹/₂" x 13¹/₂" sheets of 7 mesh plastic canvas
Worsted weight yarn
#16 tapestry needle

Stitches Used
Alternating Scotch Stitch, Backstitch, French Knot, Gobelin Stitch, Overcast Stitch, and Tent Stitch. Refer to **General Instructions**, pages 35-36, for stitch diagrams.

Instructions
Follow charts to cut and stitch Reindeer Tissue Box Cover Pieces. Using matching color Overcast Stitches, join Sides along long edges. Join Top to Sides. Referring to photo for yarn colors, cover unworked edges of Face. Tack Face to one Side.

For Bird, tack Beak and Wings to Bird pieces. Using red Overcast Stitches, join Bird pieces along unworked edges. Tack Bird to Feet. Tack Feet to Top.

Referring to photo, tack Holly pieces and Tail to tissue box cover.

Color Key
⊘	yellow
⊘	red
⊘	tan
⊘	black
⊙	black Fr. Knot

Beak
(4 x 4 threads)

Feet
(10 x 10 threads)

Wing Front
(11 x 6 threads)

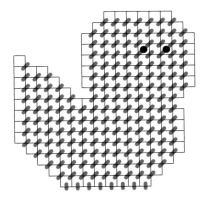

Wing Back
(11 x 6 threads)

Bird Front
(17 x 17 threads)

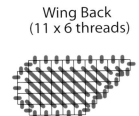

Bird Back
(17 x 17 threads)

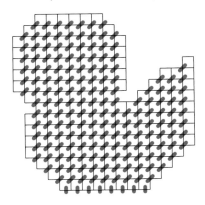

Side (30 x 37 threads) (stitch 4)

Top (30 x 30 threads)

7

Continued on page 8.

Holly (13 x 13 threads) (stitch 2)

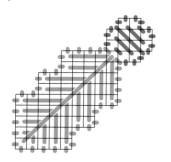

Tail (11 x 14 threads)

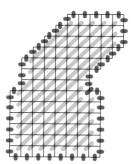

Face (42 x 56 threads)

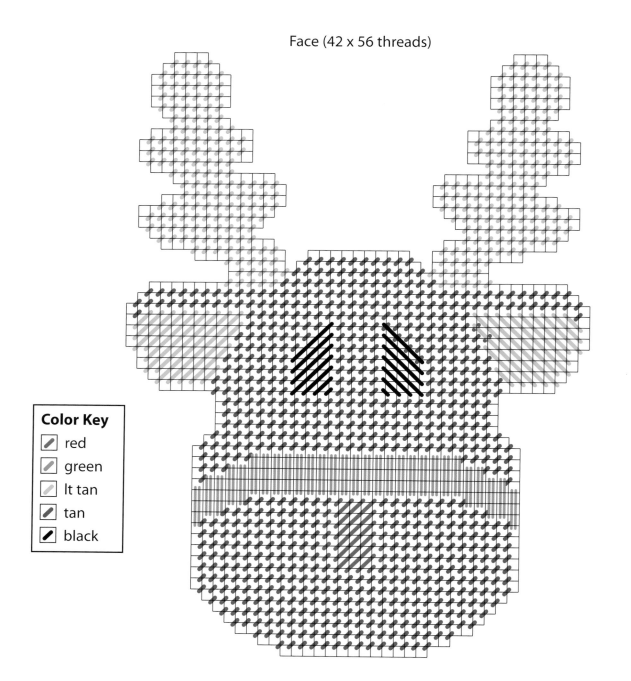

Color Key

✏	red
✏	green
✏	lt tan
✏	tan
✏	black

Sleigh Table Decoration

Size

20"w x 11"h x 7"d

Supplies

Three 10$\frac{1}{2}$" x 13$\frac{1}{2}$" sheets of 7 mesh plastic canvas
Two 3" dia. plastic canvas circle shapes
Worsted weight yarn
#16 tapestry needle
Eight wooden skewers
1 yd of $\frac{1}{8}$"wide green ribbon for reindeer
Two 8" lengths of assorted ribbon for gifts
1 yd of metallic gold cord
Four 8mm gold beads
Four $\frac{3}{8}$" gold jingle bells
Two 8mm moving eyes
$\frac{1}{4}$" pink pom-pom
Polyester fiberfill
Clear-drying craft glue

Stitches Used

Alternating Scotch Stitch, Backstitch, French Knot, Gobelin Stitch, Overcast Stitch, and Tent Stitch. Refer to **General Instructions**, pages 35-36, for stitch diagrams.

Instructions

Follow charts to cut and stitch Sleigh Table Decoration pieces. Use matching color Overcast Stitches for all joining and to cover unworked edges, unless otherwise noted.

For Sleigh, match ☆'s and ♣'s and join Bottom to Sides. Join short edges of one Runner Support along top edge of runner at ✖'s. Join remaining Runner Support along bottom edge of runner at ★'s.

9

Continued on page 10.

For Santa, join Front to Sides. Tack Arms to Sides. Tack Head to Front along edge of beard. Join Back to Sides. Glue eyes, pom-pom, Mustache, and Eyebrows to Face.

For Santa's Bag, cut circles in half. Circles are not stitched. Join one half circle to Bag at ▲'s. Tack remaining half circle to center of Bag at ✱'s. Tack Bag to Santa. Stuff Santa with fiberfill. Referring to photo, tack Santa to bottom of sleigh.

Referring to photo for yarn colors, cover unworked edges of each reindeer Face.

To assemble each reindeer, match ✖'s and join Front and Back to Body. Tack Face to Front. Tack Tail to Back. Join Bottom to Body. Thread an 8" length of ribbon through bell shank. Tie ribbon in a bow; trim ends. Glue ribbon to Reindeer.

For Bird, join Bird pieces along unworked edges. Tack Feet to Bird. Glue Wings and Beak to Bird.

Glue Heart to one reindeer. Glue Bird to one reindeer.

Use white Overcast Stitches to join Checked Gift pieces along unworked edges, forming a cube. Cover unworked edges of Green Gift. Join Blue Gift Side along short edges. Join Blue Gift Top and Bottom to Blue Gift Side along unworked edges. For each Bear, tack Bear Paws and Feet to Bear. Tack Star to Tree.

For bows on Gifts and Bears, tie an 8" length of yarn or ribbon in a bow; trim ends. Glue bows to Gifts and Bears.

Referring to photo, thread cord through Santa's mittens and through each reindeer. Tuck ends behind reindeer heads; glue in place. Glue beads to Sleigh.

Glue skewer to the wrong side of Tree, Gifts, Bears, and Candy Canes. Referring to photo, trim skewers to different lengths. Insert skewers into unstitched half circles in Santa's Bag. Adjust lengths of skewers as desired.

Sleigh Side #1 (61 x 38 threads)

10

Runner Support (22 x 6 threads) (stitch 2)

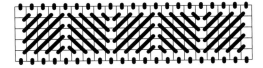

Sleigh Side #2 (61 x 38 threads)

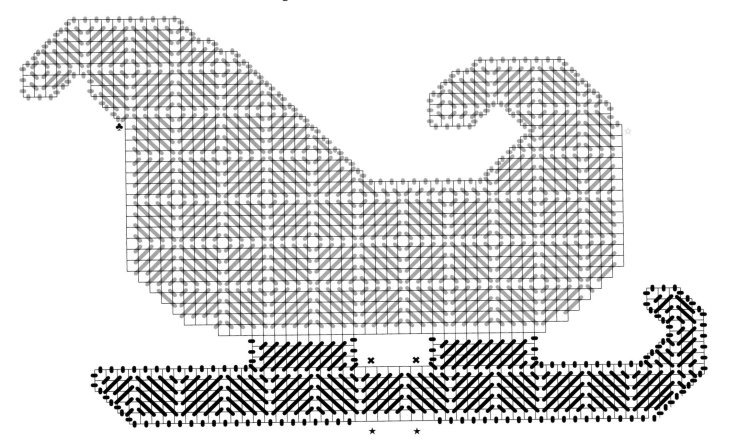

Color Key

◪	white	◪	green
◪	flesh	◪	dk red
◪	rose	◪	black
◪	red		

Santa Head (29 x 24 threads)

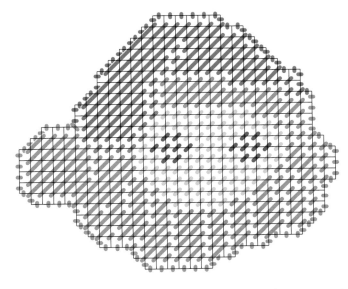

Eyebrows (4 x 3 threads each)

Mustache (10 x 4 threads)

11

Continued on page 12.

Santa Back (20 x 30 threads)

Santa Arm (18 x 14 threads)

Santa Side (13 x 70 threads)

Santa Arm (18 x 14 threads)

Santa Front (20 x 30 threads)

Blue Gift Top/Bottom (10 x 10 threads) (stitch 2)

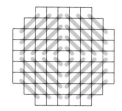

Blue Gift Side (31 x 5 threads)

Bag (44 x 17 threads)

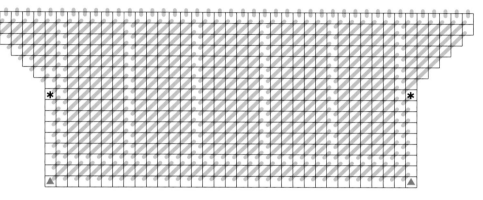

Color Key
- white
- yellow
- red
- blue
- green
- lt tan
- black

Sleigh Bottom (22 x 76 threads)

13

Continued on page 14.

Checked Gift (10 x 10 threads)
(stitch 6)

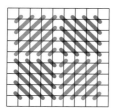

Star (10 x 10 threads)

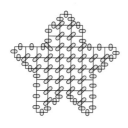

Green Gift
(8 x 20 threads)
(cut 4; stack and stitch through
all 4 layers)

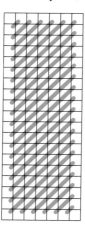

Bear Paw A
(4 x 4 threads) (stitch 2)

Bear Foot A
(5 x 6 threads) (stitch 2)

Bear A (11 x 16 threads)

Bear Paw B
(4 x 4 threads) (stitch 2)

Bear Foot B
(5 x 6 threads) (stitch 2)

Bear B (11 x 16 threads

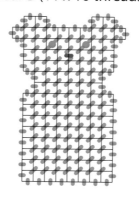

Candy Cane (11 x 20 threads)

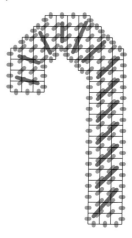

Candy Cane (11 x 20 threads)

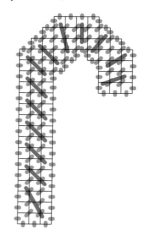

Tree (18 x 29 threads)

Color Key

- white
- yellow
- rose
- red
- green
- lt tan
- tan
- black
- blue Fr. Knot
- black Fr. Knot

Reindeer Face
(26 x 35 threads) (stitch 4)

Bird Front
(9 x 9 threads)

Bird Back
(9 x 9 threads)

Bird Beak
(3 x 3 threads)

Bird Feet
(5 x 5 threads)

Front Wing
(6 x 4 threads)

Back Wing
(6 x 4 threads)

Heart (8 x 8 threads)

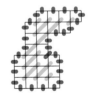

Reindeer Body
(18 x 58 threads) (stitch 4)

Reindeer Front/Back
(18 x 23 threads) (stitch 8)

Reindeer Tail
(7 x 8 threads) (stitch 4)

Reindeer Bottom
(18 x 18 threads) (stitch 4)

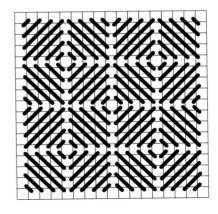

15

Reindeer Ornament

Size
2³/₄"w x 5"h x 2¹/₄"d

Supplies
One 10¹/₂" x 13¹/₂" sheet of 7 mesh plastic canvas
Worsted weight yarn
#16 tapestry needle
Clear nylon thread

Stitches Used
Alternating Scotch Stitch, Backstitch, Gobelin Stitch, Overcast Stitch, and Tent Stitch. Refer to **General Instructions**, pages 35-36, for stitch diagrams.

Instructions
Follow charts to cut and stitch Reindeer Ornament pieces.

Using matching color Overcast Stitches and matching ✖'s, join long edges of Side to Front and Back. Referring to photo for yarn colors, cover unworked edges of Face. Tack Face to Front. Tack Tail to Back.

For hanger, thread a 12" length of nylon thread through ornament; knot and trim ends.

Using black Overcast Stitches, join Bottom to Front, Back, and Side.

Color Key
- ▨ red
- ▨ green
- ▨ lt tan
- ▨ tan
- ▨ black

Face (18 x 24 threads)

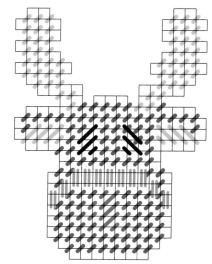

Bottom (14 x 14 threads)

Tail (6 x 7 threads)

Front/Back
(14 x 18 threads) (stitch 2)

Side (14 x 44 threads)

Santa Ornament

Size
4¹/₄"w x 4"h

Supplies
One 10¹/₂" x 13¹/₂" sheet of 7 mesh plastic canvas
Worsted weight yarn
#16 tapestry needle
Two 8mm moving eyes
¹/₄" pink pom-pom
Clear nylon thread
Clear-drying craft glue

Stitches Used
Gobelin Stitch, Overcast Stitch, and Tent Stitch. Refer to **General Instructions**, pages 35-36, for stitch diagrams.

Instructions
Follow charts to cut and stitch Santa Ornament pieces.

Using matching color Overcast Stitches, join Hat Back to Hat Front along unworked edges of Front. Tack Hat to Santa's head. Tack Eyebrows and Mustache to Santa. Glue eyes and pom-pom nose to Santa.

For hanger, thread a 12" length of nylon thread through ornament; knot and trim ends.

Color Key

▨	white	▧	red
▨	flesh	▨	dk red
▨	rose		

Santa (26 x 24 threads)

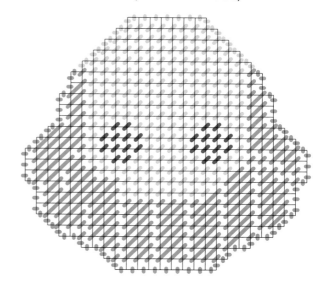

Hat Front/Back
(27 x 17 threads) (cut 2, stitch 1)

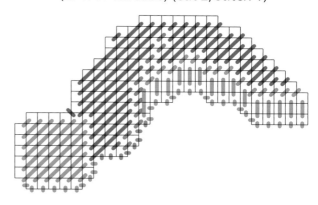

Eyebrows (4 x 3 threads each)

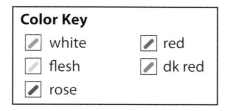

Mustache (11 x 5 threads)

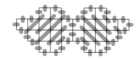

17

Christmas Lineup

Size
19"w x 15"h

Supplies
Six 10$\frac{1}{2}$" x 13$\frac{1}{2}$" sheets of 7 mesh plastic canvas
Worsted weight yarn
#16 tapestry needle
Four 3" x 10" white foam board rectangles
Six 12mm moveable eyes
One $\frac{1}{2}$" jingle bell
Three $\frac{1}{4}$" jingle bells
Six red buttons
17" length metallic gold ribbon
Four 6mm gold beads
Powder blush
Clear-drying craft glue

Stitches Used
Alternating Scotch Stitch, Backstitch, French Knot, Gobelin Stitch, Overcast Stitch, and Tent Stitch. Refer to **General Instructions**, pages 35-36, for stitch diagrams.

Reindeer
Follow charts to cut and stitch pieces, leaving shaded areas unworked. Tack Large Heart, Bow, and Head to Reindeer Front. Cut a 12" length of dk green yarn. Thread yarn through $\frac{1}{2}$" jingle bell. Insert both ends of yarn through Reindeer Head from front to back. Insert both ends of yarn back through Reindeer Head from back to front. Tie bow; trim ends. Placing foam board rectangle between Reindeer Front and Back, use matching color Overcast Stitches to join unshaded edges of Reindeer Front and Back.

Santa
Follow charts to cut and stitch pieces, leaving shaded areas unworked. Tack Nose and top edge of Mustache to Santa Front. Glue eyes to Santa Front. Glue buttons to Wreath. Tie a 9" length of red yarn in a bow; glue to Wreath. Insert Arms through Wreath; tack Arms and Wreath to Santa Front.

Matching ★'s, tack bottom edge of Hat to Santa Front. Working stitches in yellow shaded area and stitching through three layers of canvas, join Hat to Santa Front and Back. Glue Eyebrows to Hat and Santa Front. Tack Pom-pom to Hat.

Matching ♥'s, work stitches in green shaded areas through three layers of canvas to join Beard to Santa Front and Back. Matching ▲'s, tack top of Shoes to Santa Front. Place foam board rectangle between Santa Front and Back. Working stitches in blue shaded area and stitching through three layers of canvas, join Shoes to Santa Front and Back. Using matching color Overcast Stitches, join unshaded edges of Santa Front and Back. Apply blush to Santa's face.

Mrs. Santa
Follow charts to cut and stitch pieces, leaving shaded areas unworked. Tack Nose and Lace to Mrs. Santa Front. Tack Small Heart to Apron; tack Apron to Mrs. Santa Front. Tack Leaves to Hat Brim; tack Hat Brim to Mrs. Santa Front. Tack Cookies to Cookie Sheet; tack Cookie Sheet to Arms; tack Arms to Apron and Mrs. Santa Front. Glue eyes to Mrs. Santa Front.

Placing foam board rectangle between Mrs. Santa Front and Back, use matching color Overcast Stitches to join unshaded edges of Mrs. Santa Front and Back. Apply blush to Mrs. Santa's face.

Elf
Follow charts to cut and stitch pieces, leaving shaded areas unworked. Tack Nose and Ears to Elf Front. Glue eyes to Elf Front. Tack beads to Elf Front.

Using bright green Overcast Stitches, join Box Sides along short edges. Join Box Top and Bottom to Sides along long edges. Tack Box to wrong side of Arms. Tack Arms to Elf Front. Tie bow with ribbon; glue ribbon to Box, Arms, and Elf Front.

Turn Shoes over. Referring to Elf Shoes Diagram, work stitches in blue shaded areas on wrong side of Shoes. Turn piece to the right side and tack tips of Shoes to the front of the Shoes. Tack $\frac{1}{4}$" jingle bells to tips.

Matching ■'s, tack top of Shoes to Elf Front. Place foam board rectangle between Elf Front and Back. Working stitches in yellow shaded area and stitching through three layers of canvas, join Shoes to Elf Front and Back. Referring to photo for yarn colors, use Overcast Stitches to join unshaded edges of Elf Front and Back.

Tack $\frac{1}{4}$" jingle bell to tip of hat. Apply blush to Elf's face.

Joining the Characters

Work stitches in pink shaded areas to cover unworked edges of Fronts only. Insert Hinges in openings on piece sides. Work stitches in grey shaded areas to join Hinges to unworked edges of Backs only.

Color Key

- ✎ red
- ✎ green
- ◉ red Fr. Knot

Bow (17 x 10 threads)

Hinge
(14 x 7 threads) (stitch 6)

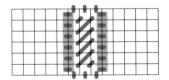

19

Continued on page 20.

Large Heart (12 x 12 threads)

Reindeer Head (30 x 55 threads)

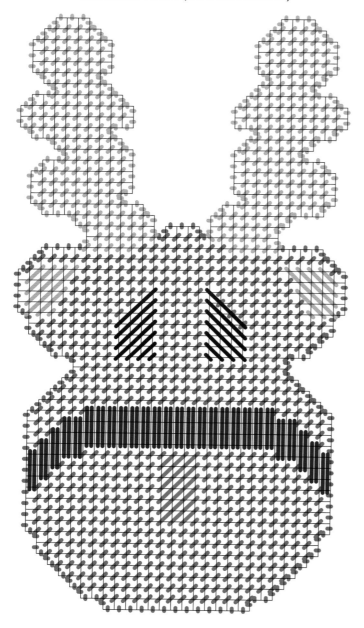

**Reindeer Front/Back
(30 x 78 threads) (cut 2) (stitch 1)**

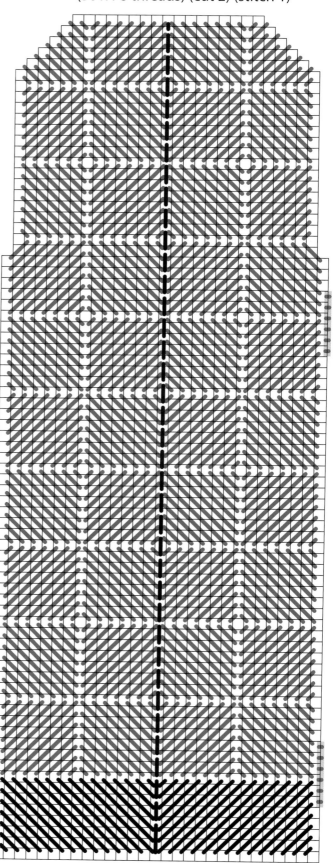

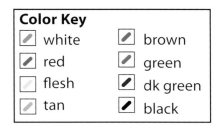

Color Key
white		brown	
red		green	
flesh		dk green	
tan		black	

Santa Eyebrows (4 x 4 threads each)

Santa Nose (4 x 4 threads) (cut 2)
Stack and stitch through two layers of canvas.

Wreath (24 x 24 threads)

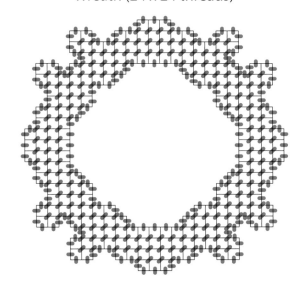

Pom-pom
(8 x 8 threads)

Mustache
(13 x 4 threads)

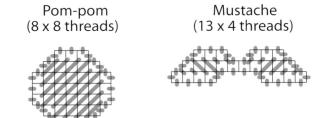

Beard (26 x 13 threads)
After working overcast stitches, tie 4" lengths of white yarn to threads to cover Beard; trim ends.

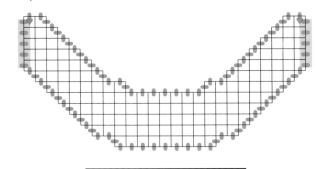

Santa Hat (27 x 19 threads)

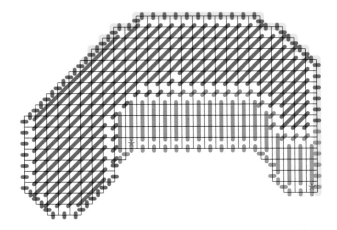

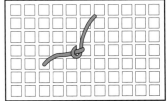

Santa Arms
(30 x 23 threads)

Santa Shoes (30 x 10 threads)

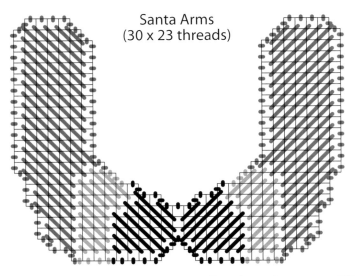

21

Continued on page 22.

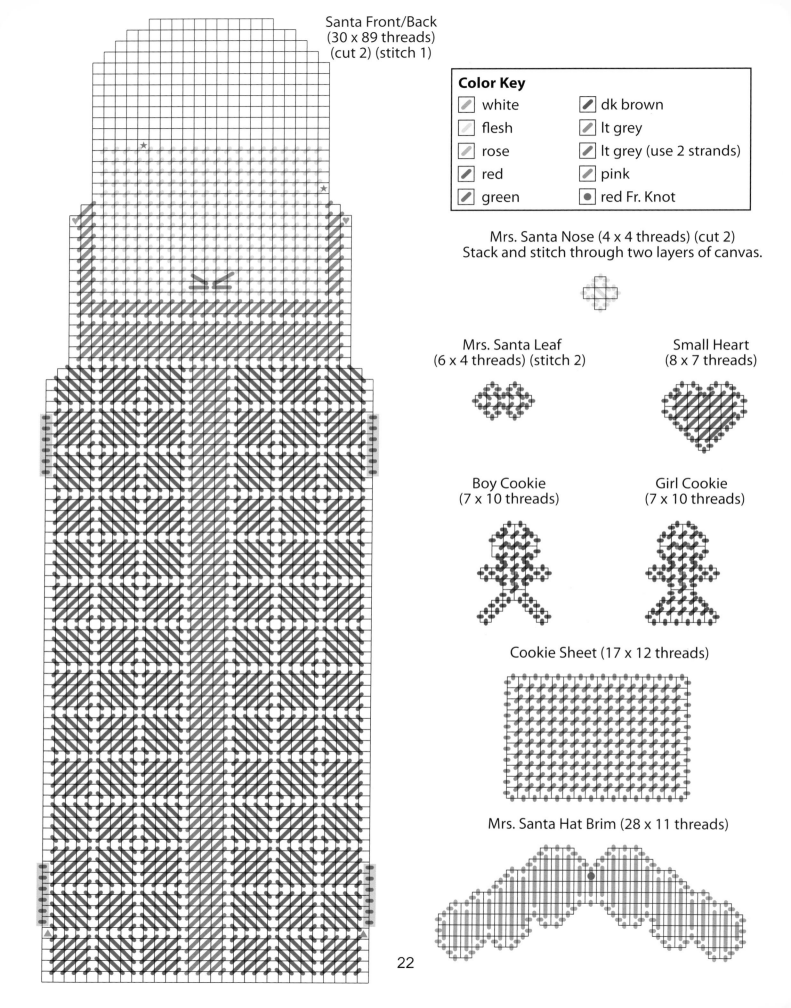

Santa Front/Back
(30 x 89 threads)
(cut 2) (stitch 1)

Color Key

white		dk brown	
flesh		lt grey	
rose		lt grey (use 2 strands)	
red		pink	
green		red Fr. Knot	

Mrs. Santa Nose (4 x 4 threads) (cut 2)
Stack and stitch through two layers of canvas.

Mrs. Santa Leaf
(6 x 4 threads) (stitch 2)

Small Heart
(8 x 7 threads)

Boy Cookie
(7 x 10 threads)

Girl Cookie
(7 x 10 threads)

Cookie Sheet (17 x 12 threads)

Mrs. Santa Hat Brim (28 x 11 threads)

22

Mrs. Santa Apron (30 x 46 threads)

Mrs. Santa Front/Back
(30 x 85 threads)
(cut 2) (stitch 1)

Mrs. Santa Lace (30 x 5 threads)

Mrs. Santa Arms (30 x 20 threads)

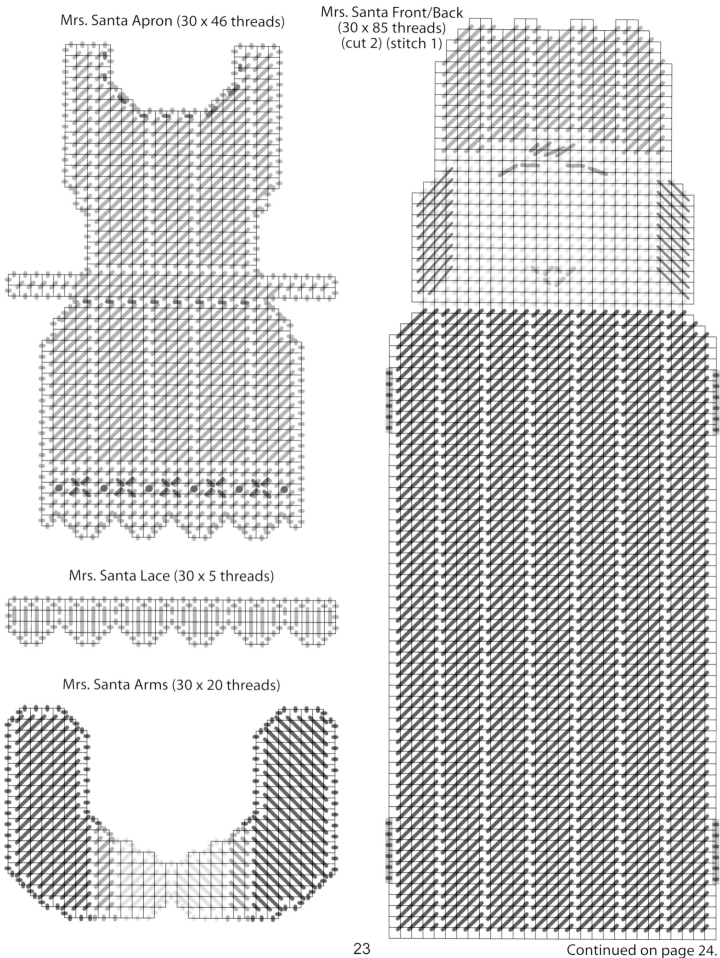

23

Continued on page 24.

Color Key

white	rose	dk red	dk green	dk brown
flesh	red	bright green	brown	black

Elf Nose (4 x 4 threads) (cut 2)
Stack and stitch through two layers of canvas.

Elf Arms (30 x 20 threads)

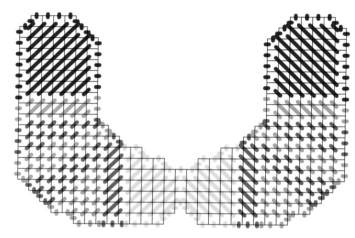

Box Side Box
(3 x 9 threads) (stitch 4)

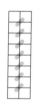

Top/Bottom
(9 x 9 threads) (stitch 2)

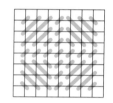

Left Elf Ear
(4 x 7 threads)

Right Elf Ear
(4 x 7 threads)

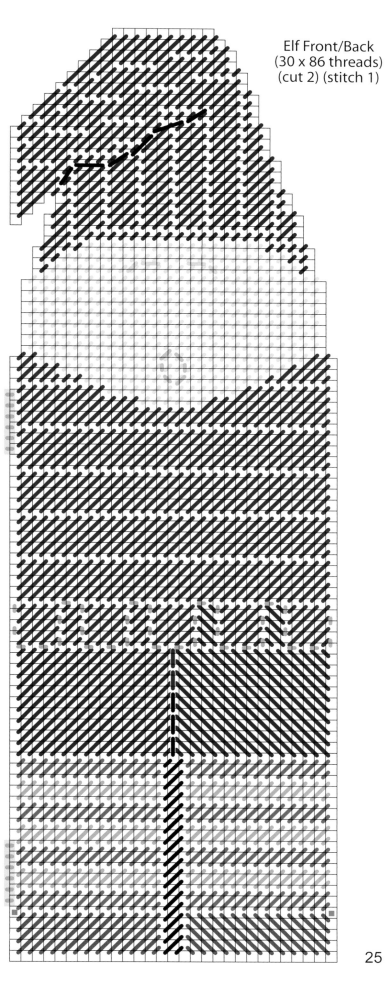

Elf Front/Back
(30 x 86 threads)
(cut 2) (stitch 1)

Elf Shoes Diagram

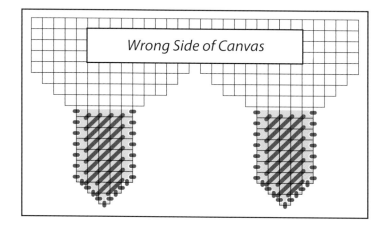

Wrong Side of Canvas

Elf Shoes (30 x 18 threads)

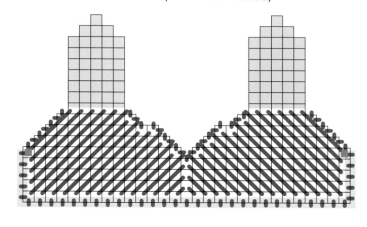

25

Snow Family Lineup

Size
20"w x 14"h

Supplies
Six 10½" x 13½" sheets of 7 mesh plastic canvas
Worsted weight yarn
#16 tapestry needle
Four 3" x 10" white foam board rectangles
Thirteen assorted buttons
Three pink silk ribbon roses
7" length of pre-strung pearls
Cardboard
Clear-drying craft glue

Stitches Used
Alternating Scotch Stitch, Backstitch, French Knot, Fringe, Gobelin Stitch, Overcast Stitch, and Tent Stitch. Refer to **General Instructions**, pages 35-36, for stitch diagrams.

Stocking Cap Snowman
Follow charts to cut and stitch pieces, leaving shaded areas unworked. Tack Eyes, edge of Nose, and Large Heart to Stocking Cap Snowman Front. Tack Scarf Tail to Scarf; tack Scarf to Stocking Cap Snowman Front. Tack Wing and Beak to Blue Bird; tack Blue Bird to Stocking Cap Snowman Front. Glue three buttons to Stocking Cap Snowman Front.

Matching ★'s, tack top and bottom edges of Hat Cuff to Stocking Cap Snowman Front. Working stitches in grey shaded areas and stitching through three layers of canvas, join Hat Cuff to Stocking Cap Snowman Front and Back.

Placing foam board rectangle between Stocking Cap Snowman Front and Back, use matching color Overcast Stitches to join unshaded edges of Stocking Cap Snowman Front and Back.

To make pom-pom for cap, cut a 4" x 3" cardboard rectangle. Cut a 5" length of red yarn. Referring to Diagram A, wrap three yards each of blue and red yarn around cardboard. Remove cardboard from yarn circle. Referring to Diagram B, tie 5" length of yarn around center of yarn circle. Clip loops of yarn circle; trim ends to shape. Tack to stocking cap.

Snowlady
Follow charts to cut and stitch pieces, leaving shaded areas unworked. Tack Eyes and edge of Nose to Snowlady Front. Glue ribbon roses to Earmuffs and Snowlady Front. Glue three buttons to Snowlady Front. Placing foam board rectangle between Snowlady Front and Back, use white Overcast Stitches to join unshaded edges of Snowlady Front and Back. Tack Earmuffs to Snowlady. For necklace, glue pearls in place.

Snow Girl
Follow charts to cut and stitch pieces, leaving shaded areas unworked. Tack Hat Cuff and edge of Nose to Snowgirl. Tack Scarf Knot to Scarf; tack Scarf to Snowgirl.

To make pom-pom for hat, cut a 3" x 2" cardboard rectangle. Cut a 5" length of pink yarn. Referring to Diagram A, wrap three yards of pink yarn around cardboard. Remove cardboard from yarn circle. Referring to Diagram B, tie 5" length of yarn around center of yarn circle. Clip loops of yarn circle; trim ends to shape. Tack pom-pom to cap.

Glue Snowgirl to Snowlady Front.

Top Hat Snowman
Follow charts to cut and stitch pieces, leaving shaded areas unworked. Tack Eyes and edge of Nose to Top Hat Snowman Front. Tack Star to Hat Brim; tack Star and Hat Brim to Top Hat Snowman Front. Tack Bow to Scarf; tack Scarf to Top Hat Snowman Front. Tack Wing and Beak to Red Bird; tack Red Bird to Top Hat Snowman Front. Glue three buttons to Top Hat Snowman Front.

Placing foam board rectangle between Top Hat Snowman Front and Back, use matching color Overcast Stitches to join unshaded edges of Top Hat Snowman Front and Back.

Diagram A   Diagram B

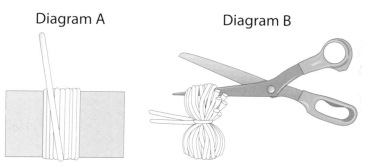

Vested Snowman

Follow charts to cut and stitch pieces, leaving shaded areas unworked. Tack Eyes, edge of Nose and Vest pieces to Vested Snowman Front. Glue two buttons to Vested Snowman Front.

Tack Beak and Wing to Little Blue Bird; tack Little Blue Bird and Small Heart to Birdhouse. Cut a 4" length of navy yarn; glue yarn ends to wrong side of Birdhouse. Tack Birdhouse to Vested Snowman Front, looping yarn over button.

Matching ■'s, use variegated blue yarn to join Hat Brim to Hat. Matching ♥s, work stitches in pink shaded area through three layers of canvas to join Hat to Vested Snowman Front and Back.

Place foam board rectangle between Vested Snowman Front and Back. Using matching color Overcast Stitches, join unshaded edges of Vested Snowman Front and Back.

Joining the Characters

Work stitches in blue shaded areas to cover unworked edges of Fronts only. Insert Hinges in openings on piece sides. Work stitches in green shaded areas to join Hinges to unworked edges of Backs only.

Continued on page 28.

Color Key

✏ white		✏ lt blue	
✏ yellow		✏ blue	
✏ orange		✏ black	
✏ pink		● black Fr. Knot	
✏ red		○ red fringe	
✏ purple		○ blue fringe	

Stocking Cap Snowman Hat Cuff (30 x 11 threads)

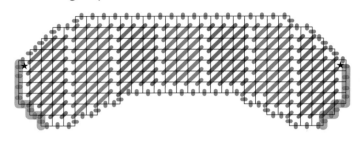

Hinge (14 x 7 threads) (stitch 6)

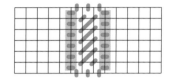

Blue Bird (17 x 17 threads)

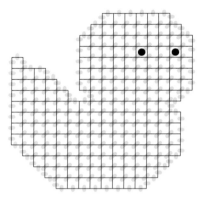

Blue Bird Beak (4 x 4 threads)

Stocking Cap Snowman Nose (7 x 4 threads)

Stocking Cap Snowman Eye (4 x 4 threads) (stitch 2)

Blue Bird Wing (11 x 6 threads)

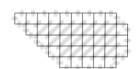

Large Heart (8 x 8 threads)

Stocking Cap Snowman Scarf (30 x 9 threads)

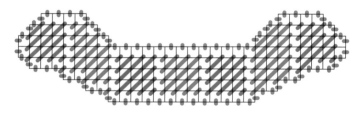

Stocking Cap Snowman Scarf Tails (15 x 13 threads)

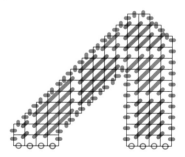

Stocking Cap Snowman Front/Back
(30 x 86 threads) (cut 2) (stitch 1)

Snowgirl Hat Cuff
(13 x 4 threads)

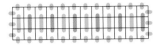

Snowgirl
(12 x 39 threads)

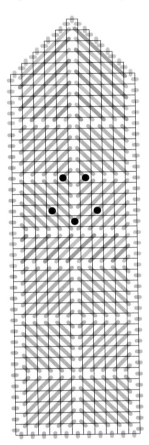

Snowgirl Nose
(5 x 3 threads)

Snowgirl Scarf Knot
(4 x 4 threads)

Snowgirl Scarf Tails
(9 x 12 threads)

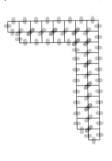

29

Continued on page 30.

Snowlady Front/Back
(30 x 78 threads) (cut 2) (stitch 1)

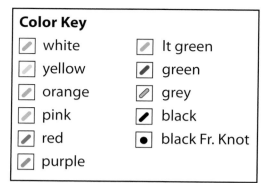

Color Key

▨ white		▨ lt green	
▨ yellow		▨ green	
▨ orange		▨ grey	
▨ pink		▨ black	
▨ red		● black Fr. Knot	
▨ purple			

Snowlady Eye
(4 x 4 threads) (stitch 2)

Snowlady Nose
(7 x 4 threads)

Snowlady Earmuffs
(8 x 52 threads)

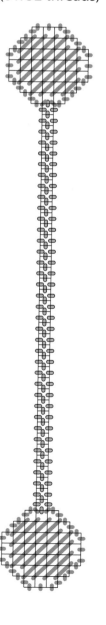

30

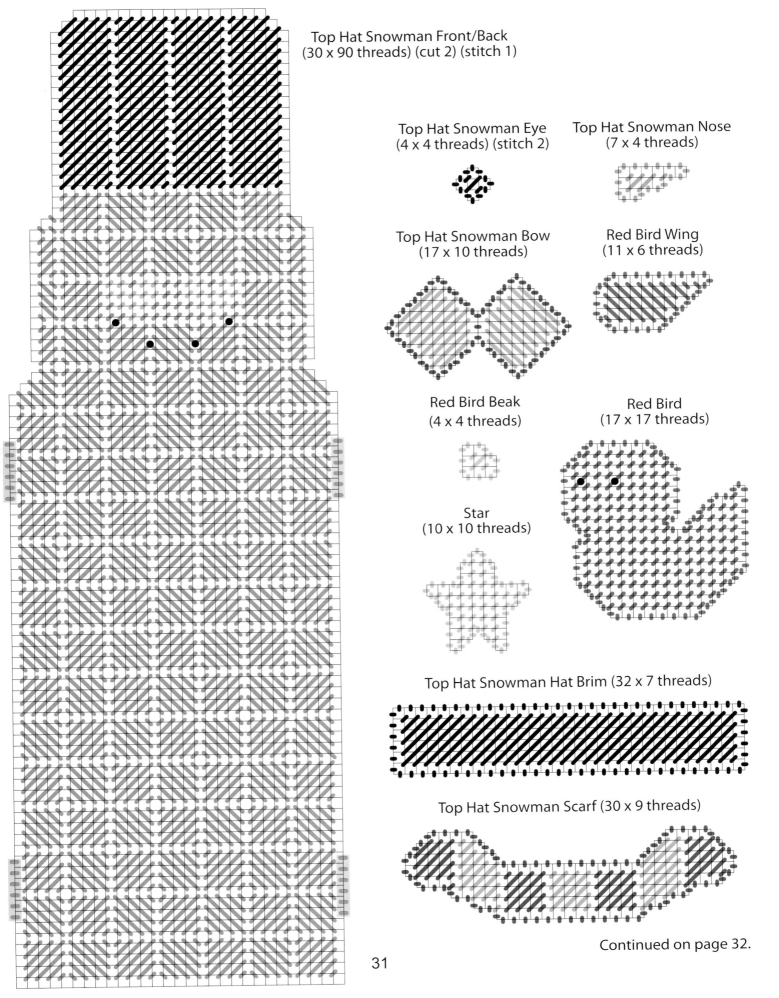

Top Hat Snowman Front/Back
(30 x 90 threads) (cut 2) (stitch 1)

Top Hat Snowman Eye
(4 x 4 threads) (stitch 2)

Top Hat Snowman Nose
(7 x 4 threads)

Top Hat Snowman Bow
(17 x 10 threads)

Red Bird Wing
(11 x 6 threads)

Red Bird Beak
(4 x 4 threads)

Red Bird
(17 x 17 threads)

Star
(10 x 10 threads)

Top Hat Snowman Hat Brim (32 x 7 threads)

Top Hat Snowman Scarf (30 x 9 threads)

Continued on page 32.

Color Key

▨ white	▨ orange	▨ red	▨ variegated blue	▨ brown	● black Fr. Knot
▨ yellow	▨ pink	▨ lt blue	▨ navy	▨ black	

Vested Snowman Eye
(4 x 4 threads) (stitch 2)

Vested Snowman Nose
(7 x 4 threads)

Small Heart
(6 x 5 threads)

Little Blue Bird Beak
(3 x 3 threads)

Little Blue Bird
(9 x 9 threads)

Little Blue Bird Wing
(6 x 4 threads)

Birdhouse (20 x 24 threads)

Vested Snowman Hat (26 x 15 threads)

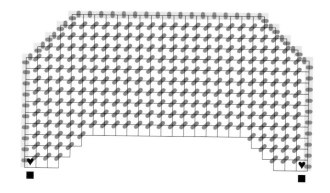

32

Vested Snowman Hat Brim (29 x 8 threads)

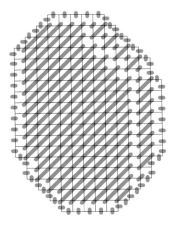

Vest Left Side
(14 x 19 threads)

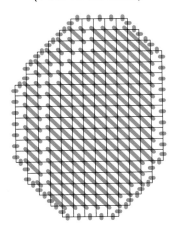

Vest Right Side
(14 x 19 threads)

Vested Snowman Front/Back
(30 x 82 threads) (cut 2) (stitch 1)

33

General Instructions

Working with Plastic Canvas

Counting Threads. The lines of the canvas are referred to as threads. Before cutting out the pieces, note the thread count of each chart listed above the chart, indicating the number of threads in the width and height. To cut plastic canvas pieces accurately, count **threads** (not **holes**) as shown in **Fig. 1**.

Fig. 1

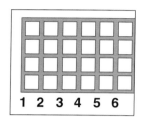

Marking the Canvas. You may use an overhead projector pen to mark the canvas. Outline shape with pen, cut out shape, and remove markings before stitching.

Cutting the Canvas. Cut as close to the thread as possible without cutting into the thread. If you don't cut close enough, "nubs" or "pickets" will be left on the edge. Make sure to cut all nubs from the canvas before stitching because nubs will snag the yarn and are difficult to cover. A craft knife is helpful when cutting a small area from the center of a larger piece of canvas. When using a craft knife, protect the table below with a layer of cardboard.

When cutting canvas along a diagonal, cut through the center of each intersection. This will leave enough plastic canvas on both sides of the cut so that both pieces may be used. Properly cut diagonal corners will be less likely to snag yarn and are easier to cover.

Working with Worsted Weight Yarn

Most brands have plies which are twisted together to form one strand. When the instructions indicate two plies of yarn, separate the strand of yarn and stitch using only two of the plies.

Reading the Color Key

A color key is included for each project, indicating the color used for each stitch on the chart. Additional information may also be included, such as the number of plies to use when working a particular stitch.

Reading the Chart

When possible, the drawing on the chart looks like the completed stitch. For example, the tent stitches on the chart are drawn diagonally across an intersection of threads just as they look on the piece. When a stitch cannot be clearly drawn on the chart, like a French Knot, a symbol will be used instead.

Stitching the Design

Securing the First and Last Stitches. Don't knot the end of your yarn before you begin stitching. Instead, begin each length of yarn by coming up from the wrong side of the canvas and leaving a 1"-2" tail on the wrong side. Hold this tail against the canvas and work the first few stitches over the tail. When secure, clip the tail close to the stitched piece. Long tails can become tangled in future stitches or can show through to the right side of the canvas. After all the stitches of one color in an area are complete, end by running the needle under several stitches on the back. Trim the end close to the stitched piece.

Using Even Tension. Keep your stitching tension consistent, with each stitch lying flat and even. Pulling or yanking the yarn causes the tension to be too tight, and you will be able to see through your project. If the tension is too loose, the stitches won't lie flat. Most stitches tend to twist yarn. Drop your needle and let the yarn untwist occasionally.

Joining Pieces

Straight Edges. To join two or more pieces along a straight edge, place one piece on top of the other with right or wrong sides together. Make sure the edges are even, then overcast the pieces together through all layers.

Shaded Areas. Shaded areas usually mean that all the stitches in that area are used to join pieces of canvas. Do not work these stitches until the project instructions say you should.

Tacking. To tack pieces, run your needle under the backs of some stitches on one stitched piece to secure the yarn. Then run the needle through the canvas or under stitches on the piece to be tacked in place. This should securely attach pieces without tacking stitches showing.

Uneven Edges. When you join a diagonal edge to a straight edge, the holes will not line up exactly. Keep the pieces even and stitch through the holes as many times as necessary to completely cover the canvas.

Stitch Diagrams

Unless otherwise indicated, bring needle up at **1** and all **odd** numbers and down at **2** and all **even** numbers.

Backstitch

This stitch is worked over completed stitches to outline or define **(Fig. 2)**. It is sometimes worked over more than one thread. It can also be used to cover canvas **(Fig. 3)**.

Fig. 2

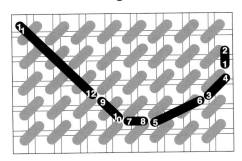

Fig. 3

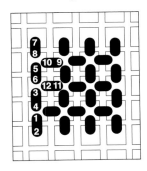

French Knot

Come up at 1. Wrap yarn once around needle. Insert the needle at 2 and pull it through the canvas, holding the yarn until it must be released **(Fig. 4)**.

Fig. 4

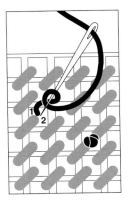

Fringe Stitch

Fold a length of yarn in half. Thread needle with loose ends of yarn. Bring needle up at 1, leaving a 1" loop on the back of the canvas. Bring needle around the edge of canvas and through loop **(Fig. 5)**. Pull to tighten loop **(Fig. 6)**. Trim fringe to desired length. A dot of glue on back of fringe will help keep stitch in place.

Fig. 5

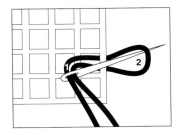

Fig. 6

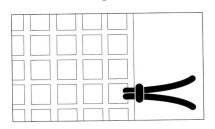

35

Gobelin Stitch

This straight stitch is worked over two or more threads or intersections **(Fig. 7)**. The number of threads or intersections may vary according to the chart.

Fig. 7

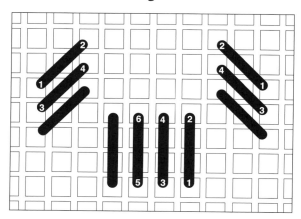

Tent Stitch

This stitch is worked in horizontal or vertical rows over one intersection **(Fig. 9)**. Refer to **Fig. 10** to work the reversed tent stitch.

Fig. 9

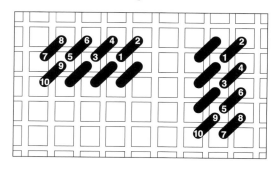

Fig. 10

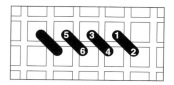

Overcast Stitch

This stitch covers the edge of canvas and joins pieces **(Fig. 8)**. It may be necessary to go through the same hole more than once to get even coverage on the edge, especially at the corners.

Fig. 8

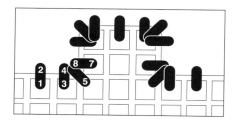

We have made every effort to ensure that these instructions are accurate and complete. We cannot, however, be responsible for human error, typographical mistakes, or variations in individual work.